Exploring Mars

The Red Planet

Darleen Ramos

Contents

Rigby
A Harcourt Achieve Imprint

www.Rigby.com
1-800-531-5015

Blast Off to Mars!

Three, two, one, liftoff! Your space ship is roaring as it blasts into outer space. You peer through the window and see the deep, blue ocean waters and the green plants of Earth. There is no time to think about home, because you must think about your purpose. After all, you are going to land on Mars, the red planet! No humans have ever walked on Mars!

What will it be like to explore Mars? Grab your space helmet, and get ready to go exploring!

3

When you come close to Mars, you will notice the red color of the soil. This red color comes from the iron that is mixed in the sand and rocks. The windy, dry planet also has many sand dunes and dust storms. On the surface, you will also see many rocks and **craters.** Craters are large holes in the surface caused by crashing **meteorites,** or rocks that fall from space.

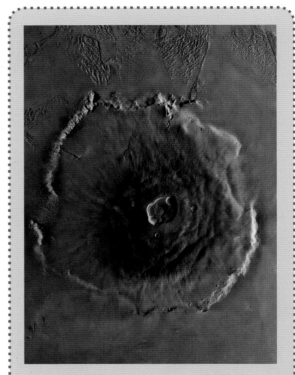

This is what the surface of Mars looks like.

As you search for your landing site, you will see huge volcanoes and deep canyons. The largest volcano on Mars is Olympus Mons. It is also the largest volcano in our solar system. This giant volcano is three times higher than Mount Everest, which is the highest mountain on Earth.

Did You Know?

- In the middle of Mars there is a deep crack in the surface, called Mariner Valley.
- Mariner Valley is the longest and deepest valley in the solar system.
- Mariner Valley is over 3,000 miles long. On Earth, it would be the length of the United States, from coast to coast!
- Mariner Valley is about four times deeper than the Grand Canyon.

The Weather

The average temperature on Mars is below 32°F. In the summer, temperatures barely reach 15°F. At night, the temperature drops to 110°F below zero! The winter months are so cold that the air turns to ice. *Brrrr!*

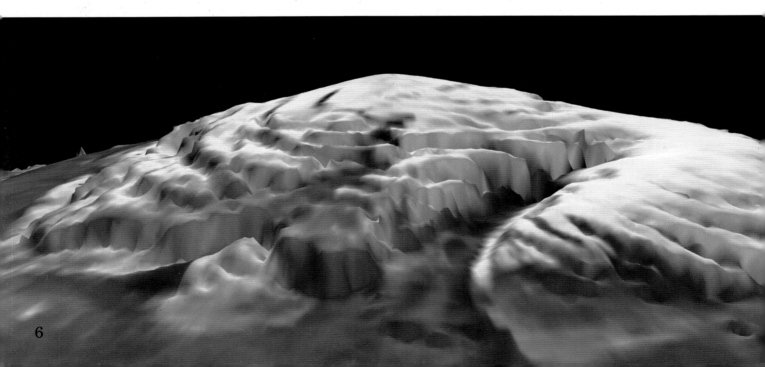

Did You Know That Mars Has Moons?

There are two small moons that circle Mars. The moons of Mars are much smaller than our moon. If you look at them when you are on Mars, the moons will look like bright stars in the sky.

Learning About Mars

It may be your dream to really travel to Mars, but long ago, people didn't know all of this about Mars. They could see only a few planets because they did not have **telescopes,** which would have helped them see things that were far away.

The ancient Romans were one group of people who watched the sky at night. They could see one planet that had a gleaming red glow. The red color reminded them of war, so they decided to name this planet Mars. Mars was the Roman god of war.

Early **astronomers** were just as curious about Mars as we are today. These scientists who studied outer space thought Mars was strange because it was red and because it moved in a different direction than all of the other planets. A scientist named Galileo wanted to know why.

Galileo was a scientist who studied Mars.

In 1609 Galileo built his own powerful telescope, which he used to look at Mars. At that time people believed that Earth was the center of the universe. By looking at Mars with his telescope, Galileo helped prove that the sun is the center of our **solar system**. He also proved that the planets, including Earth, **revolve** around the sun. That means that the planets move around the sun.

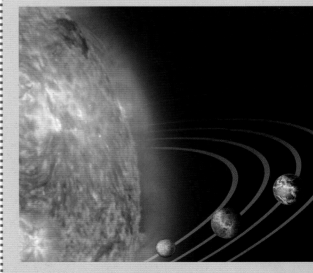

All of the planets revolve around the sun.

10

Astronomers hoped to find living creatures on Mars. They hoped that telescopes would help them. Would Mars have life?

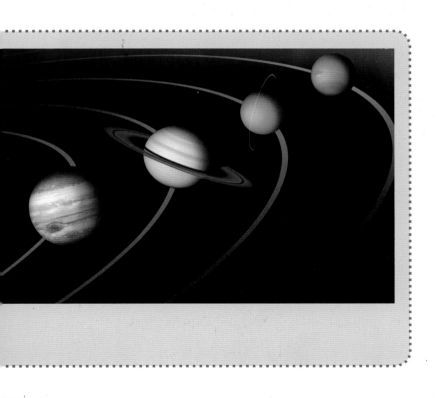

Stories About Martians

Space travelers today may not be afraid of Martians, but in 1877, people were very afraid. An Italian astronomer claimed that he saw dark lines on the surface of Mars. He called the lines *canali*. People thought the astronomer meant that there were canals on Mars. They thought that someone living on Mars had built them!

This is a canal on Earth.

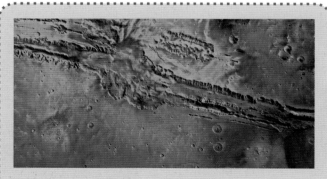

This is a *canali* on Mars.

Another American astronomer also believed there were canals on Mars. He said that the canals were built by Martians who wanted to water their dry farmlands. Scientists disagreed with this astronomer, but people were interested in his stories.

Science Fiction and Martians

After the astronomer's stories were heard, writers started describing little green men who lived on Mars. One famous fiction story was *The War of the Worlds,* written by H.G. Wells in 1898. He described Martians as horrible creatures who wanted to attack Earth.

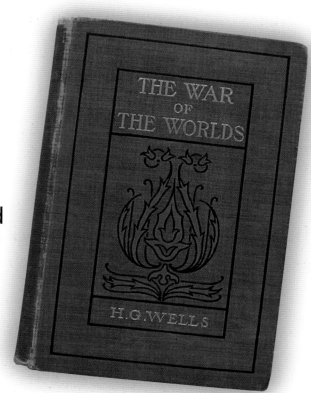

People thought this story was real.

Forty years later, the story was told on the radio by Orson Welles, a famous movie director. Listeners thought the story was real and ran from their homes, terrified that they were under attack.

Like they did in the past, people today continue to write about Martians. Books and movies describe Martians as both friendly creatures and as enemies. Some stories suggest that people from Earth live on Mars. Today we know this isn't true.

In 1938, Orson Welles read *The War of the Worlds* on the radio.

Looking for Life on Mars

As time passed, telescopes improved, but the view of Mars was still fuzzy. Astronomers needed clear photos, and they got what they wanted in 1965 when the *Mariner 4* spacecraft flew near Mars. They saw that Mars was more like Earth's moon than it was like Earth.

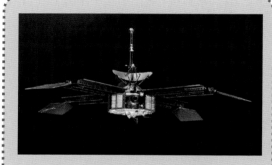

Photos proved that there were no canals, no water, and no plants on Mars.

Before they saw the photos of Mars, people thought that Mars was comparable to Earth. Now we know that these two planets are very different. Mars is 142 million miles away from the sun, and Earth is 91 million miles away. Mars has two moons, and Earth has one. On Mars there is not enough **oxygen** for humans to breathe.

Comparing Earth and Mars

	Earth	Mars
Length of a Day	24 hours	24 hours and 37 minutes
Length of a Year	365 days	687 days

Exploring Mars

Mariner 9 was the first spacecraft sent into outer space to go around Mars. It took pictures of dry river channels that cannot be seen with a telescope.

Mariner 9 took pictures of the surface of Mars.

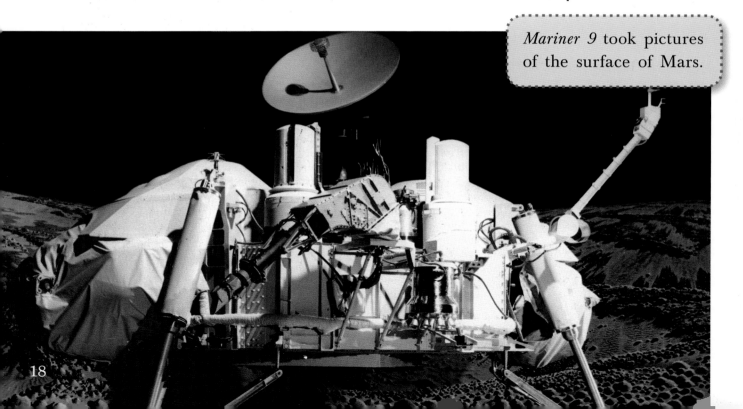

The photographs were great, but they couldn't prove that there was life on Mars. Scientists wanted to know more about the planet's surface, so in 1976, the *Viking* landers were launched. The landers took pictures and tested some of the soil. Scientists wanted to know if anything was living in the soil. Nothing was. The landers also studied the weather. They found that the weather on Mars consists of either light winds or dust storms.

The Viking landers took these pictures in 1976.

Robots on Mars

The *Viking* landers couldn't move, but they had arms that dug up the soil that was tested. Scientists wanted to send a **rover,** which could travel around the planet. People on Earth would steer the rover.

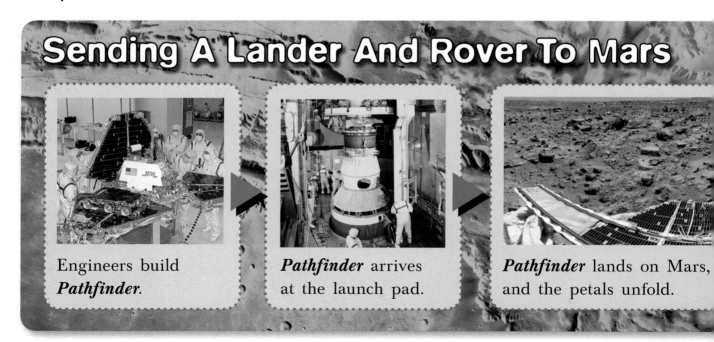

Sending A Lander And Rover To Mars

Engineers build *Pathfinder*.

Pathfinder arrives at the launch pad.

Pathfinder lands on Mars, and the petals unfold.

On July 4, 1997, the spaceship *Pathfinder* landed on Mars with our first rover, *Sojourner,* which rolled off the ramp onto the surface of Mars. It moved very slowly over the rocky surface. Scientists were very excited when they saw the pictures of Earth's first robot on another planet.

Sojourner rolls down the ramp.

Sojourner explores Mars and sends reports back to Earth.

Robots and Rovers

Sojourner helped scientists learn a lot about Mars. The rover discovered surface features on Mars that look like features found on Earth. *Sojourner* also found some round pebbles. Pebbles are formed on Earth by running water. Finding the pebbles might prove that Mars once had water.

Sojourner was Earth's first robot on another planet.

Sojourner: The Robot

- *Sojourner* is about the size of a child's small wagon.
- *Sojourner* has 6 wheels and legs that move.
- *Sojourner* can test soil and rocks for minerals.

The *Spirit* and *Opportunity* rovers landed on Mars in early 2004. Their simple mission was to find out if water has ever flowed on Mars.

One day you might actually get to visit Mars. Will you be an astronaut who examines the red rocks and looks at the red sky? How will you feel? What will you think? What will you discover?

Opportunity Rover

Spirit Rover taking picture.

Glossary

astronomer a person who studies the stars, planets, and space

crater a hole made by a large rock that crashes onto the surface of a planet

meteorite a piece of rock from outer space that hits the surface of a moon or a planet

oxygen one of the gases in the air that is necessary for humans to breathe

revolve move around

rover a remote-controlled cart

solar system a group of planets and other objects that move around a star, such as our sun. Our solar system has planets, asteroids, meteoroids, and comets.

telescope an instrument used to make objects that are far away look closer and bigger